I0481792

Passive Income

Passive Income Tutorial with 7 Online Ideas to Generate Passive Income Streams for Beginners

LELA GIBSON

Copyright © 2017 Lela Gibson

All rights reserved.

CONTENTS

Introduction

I want to thank you and congratulate you for buying the book, *"Passive Income - Passive Income Tutorial with 7 Online Ideas to Generate Passive Income Streams for Beginners."* This book contains proven steps and strategies on how to generate passive income.

Passive income refers to making money while you sleep. You can put your money to work and add an extra sum to your monthly income. Having a passive income is extremely important, as you cannot depend on your salary all your life. There will come a time when you will have to retire and require money to lead a normal life. Once you get your passive income going, it can serve as your retirement money.

The money can also be saved for long-term and short-term expenses. You can use the money to fulfill your wishes such as funding your child's education, taking vacations, buying big ticket items, etc. There are many choices to pick from when it comes to passive income, and you can choose one that gives you a consistent stream of income.

This book will guide you through the different options that are available and how you can put them to work at the earliest! You will find one topic discussed per chapter making it easy to navigate through them and make the most of your investments.

Thanks again for buying this book, I hope you enjoy it!

© **Copyright 2017 by Lela Gibson - All rights reserved.**

This document is geared towards providing exact and reliable information in regards to the topic and issue covered. The publication is sold with the idea that the publisher is not required to render accounting, officially permitted, or otherwise, qualified services. If advice is necessary, legal or professional, a practiced individual in the profession should be ordered.

- From a Declaration of Principles which was accepted and approved equally by a Committee of the American Bar Association and a Committee of Publishers and Associations.

In no way is it legal to reproduce, duplicate, or transmit any part of this document in either electronic means or in printed format. Recording of this publication is strictly prohibited and any storage of this document is not allowed unless with written permission from the publisher. All rights reserved.

The information provided herein is stated to be truthful and consistent, in that any liability, in terms of inattention or otherwise, by any usage or abuse of any policies, processes, or directions contained within is the solitary and utter responsibility of the recipient reader. Under no circumstances will any legal responsibility or blame be held against the publisher for any reparation, damages, or monetary loss due to the information herein, either directly or indirectly.

Respective authors own all copyrights not held by the publisher.

The information herein is offered for informational purposes solely, and is universal as so. The presentation of the information is without contract or any type of guarantee assurance.

The trademarks that are used are without any consent, and the publication of the trademark is without permission or backing by the trademark owner. All trademarks and brands within this book are for clarifying purposes only and are the owned by the owners themselves, not affiliated with this document.

Chapter 1: Stock Market Investments

When it comes to setting up a passive income business, one of the go-to choices is stock market investment.

The stock market is a vast place where every day, thousands of stocks are bought and sold. These stocks refer to shares of companies who float them into the market to get people to buy them. Say you buy 200 stocks of Microsoft. This makes you part owner of the company limited to the percentage of shares that you hold.

There are two types of markets namely physical markets and virtual markets. Physical markets, like NYSE, are where traders and brokers buy and sell stocks on the floor of the market. Virtual markets, like NASDAQ, are those where investors directly buy and sell stocks over the Internet.

Before you get started with stock market investments, there are a few things that you must do, which are discussed as follows.

- First off, you must buy a computer system that you will exclusively use to trade in the market.
- You will need a fast Internet connection that will let you keep up with the trade.
- You should sign up with a brokerage firm who will permit you to use their account in the market to buy and sell stocks. Go through the different brokerage firms that exist and pick one that charges the least amount of brokerage fees.
- You will have to hire a broker to help you buy and sell the stocks. This is especially important if you are new to the world of stocks and do not know how to go about it. Once you gain the confidence, you can buy and sell stocks on your own.
- You can install the software that is required to carry out trade in the stock

market. The brokerage firm usually supplies this software, or you can download it from an online source.

- Create a Watchlist and add in different stocks that you would like to keep an eye on. Keeping an eye on the stocks will help you make better investments and safeguard your money.
- Research is key. You have to pick five stocks from each sector and keep an eye on them for at least a month to be able to judge whether they make good choices.

There are many types of stock market instruments to choose from, and some are discussed as follows.

Stocks

Two main types of stocks exist in the market namely equity and preferred. Equity stocks are those that are readily available in the market. They entitle the owner with voting rights in the company. They will also receive a profit or dividend depending on how much the company makes. However, these will be considered last in case a company winds up.

Preferred shares are given out to company employees, board members, etc. These are not readily available in the market and will only be up for sale if one of the owners decides to give up his share. Owners of such shares are entitled to a fixed sum per month. Their interest will be considered first in case the company winds up. However, they will not have the right to vote for the board of directors.

Once you buy the stocks of a company, you can treat them as long-term stocks or short-term stocks. Short-term stocks are those that you hold for a week or less. In fact, you can hold them for a single day and dispose of them. By doing so, you stand to gain daily profits and can reduce the sum of brokerage that you pay out.

However, it might take some time for you to understand how the market works and wait for a few days before taking up intraday investments.

If you develop the confidence to trade intraday, then you can look to scalp trading where you buy and sell stocks within a few seconds.

Forex

Forex refers to foreign exchange. As you know, each country has its currency, and not all are valued at the same price. There will be a few weaker ones and some strong ones. As a forex trader, you have to find the weaker ones and exchange them for the stronger ones and vice versa. Some strong currencies include the Australian dollar, Canadian dollar, US dollar, Japanese Yen and Euro. These are universal and can be bought and sold in any part of the world. The forex market is open 24 hours a day, and you can buy and sell currency pairs on any stock exchange.

Precious metals

Precious metals are those that are bought and sold in the bullion market. Right from gold to silver to platinum, there are many options to pick from. You can choose whatever suits you best. Silver is cheaper than gold and gold is less expensive than platinum. You need not get physical possession of these metals and can buy and sell them on an intraday basis.

Commodities Futures

Just like precious metals, commodities are also traded on the market. These include the likes of potatoes, cotton, rice, wheat, onions, etc. As an investor, you are required to determine the future price that these commodities will be valued at. If you get it right then, you stand to gain from your prediction. You will have to guess within a stipulated period.

Options

Options are those that give the trader an option to go ahead with a deal or forgo it. Say Mr. A offers you 500 shares of a company at $5 per share. You reserve the shares by paying a sum of $100 and promise to pay the rest in a week's time. During the week, if the price of the share rises to $8, then you stand to gain from the deal. Mr. A will be forced to sell the share at $5 owing to the promise he has made. On the other hand, if the price drops to $3 then you are bound to make a loss on the deal. In such a case, you can refuse to go through with the deal or wait till one week for the deal to automatically expire. You will lose the $100 you paid to reserve the stocks but will escape a significant loss.

Mutual funds

Mutual funds are long-term investments that people use to increase their money's worth over the course of many years. Once you pay the money, a fund manager will pool in your money along with other investors' money and invest it in a scheme. You will be allotted a unit that will contain a combination of financial instruments. You cannot withdraw your investment until the deal reaches maturity. You can only check your net worth on a daily basis.

As you can see, there are many investment options to pick from, and you can choose whatever suits you best.

Chapter 2 Writing

The writing job is one of the most lucrative in the world of passive income. You can write eBooks or go the old-fashioned way and publish books.

Here is a look at both these options in detail.

eBooks

EBooks are electronic books that can be downloaded and read on smartphones and tablets. They are now slowly replacing regular books and will soon overtake them in popularity. You can write eBooks and sell them on platforms such as Amazon. Amazon has a large customer base and will make it quite easy for you to sell your books. You can choose any of their programs and put your book on sale within a day or two. But remember that there will be strict competition, and so, you will have to write a good book that gives your audience unique information. There is no limit to the number of books that can be published and you can write on as many topics as you like. You can publicize the book using your social media accounts so that people know about it and buy your book.

Blogs and content

If you think it is tedious to write an entire book and would like to write just short articles, then you can consider writing blog posts. Create a free account on Blogger or WordPress and start writing on topics that interest the masses. You can use it to write on trending topics and get more people to like your posts. Make use of social media to popularize the blogs. The idea is to generate a huge traffic so that you can use the viewership to your advantage. Again, you have to write unique content so that you can capture a larger audience.

You can also feature as a writer for other people's blogs. There will be many such jobs available where companies will pay you for writing blogs for them. You can go to a website such as Freelancer.com or Upwork.com to find blogging jobs. You can choose from getting paid per article to pay per click. Big sites such as Forbes.com pay you $5 for 1,000 clicks. The more the number of articles you put out, the more money you make.

Apart from blogs, you can also do content writing for websites. There are many topics to choose from, and you can write on a topic that you are comfortable with. Make sure you pick topics that are trending and sure to become popular. You have to find clients looking for writers and allot at least an hour every day to write the posts.

Here are some of the requisites for making it big in the world of blogging.

- First off, you have to build a large audience base. It is this audience that will help you make money through your blogs. You have to actively involve your customers and make sure you get them to subscribe to your blogs. Have them on your email list so that you can send them emails about your latest work and get them to visit your blog posts more often. On average, you have to have at least 10,000+ active readers who will help you keep your blogs active.

- Keep up with the trends. Pick out topics that are hot and trending. Make use of hashtags to make it easier for people to find you and the subjects you write on. Remember that the content has to be unique and appealing and good enough to keep your audience glued and wanting more.

- Consistency is key. Maintain relevance between the different topics that you cover on your blog. It should inspire your audience and give them something to take back after reading your posts.

- You should make use of affiliate marketing. The concept deals with using your blog to find companies who are willing to advertise on your blog. You can make money by hosting them. We will discuss this topic in detail in a future chapter of this book.

Publishing

If you are keen on going the old-fashioned way, then consider publishing your book. For this, you must find a publisher who is willing to publish your book. There will be many, and each one will offer a different payment scheme. You can choose whatever suits you best. It can take anywhere from a few weeks to a few months to find a publisher willing to publish your books. In the meantime, you can work on your book and make it as appealing as possible. Once you find the publisher, you must talk out the terms with them and agree on a selling price for the book. You must also discuss the fee they will receive for publishing your work.

Once published, you must hold press conferences and promote your book as much as you can. It is the only way in which you can get people to notice it and push its sales. Some publishers also offer advertising services at discounted rates, which can prove to be a good option for you.

If you already have a successful blog or website, then you will find it relatively easy to find a publisher. You can also make use of your blog or website to publicize about your book and get your existing audience to read and draw in other customers.

Chapter 3 YouTube

YouTube started out as a platform where people shared their videos for the world to see. Today, it has grown in size and become one of the most used websites in the world and a preferred choice for setting up a passive income business. With thousands of people using it to gain online popularity, YouTube is now a worldwide phenomenon.

If you wish to make the most of the opportunity provided by YouTube, then here are some things that you can do to get started with it on the right foot.

Set up a channel

The very first thing that you will require is a channel that you can use to host the videos. The channel will act as your portal to connect with your audience. You can make your channel as unique as possible. First off, upload a picture that best describes your channel. You can put up a picture of yourself or your company's logo. Once your channel is up, you can use it to subscribe to others that you admire or would like to follow. You can share details of your channel on your social media website to get people to like it and subscribe to it.

Making videos

The next step is to make videos to upload to your channel. The main aim of using YouTube is to make unique videos that people will love to see. There are many topics to choose from such as reviews, opinions, unboxing, tutorials, DIYs, etc. Once you make the video and upload it, you have to show it to a test audience comprising of friends and family. Ask them to be critical about it so that you can make it exciting and appealing to a larger audience. Make sure you make use of a good quality camera and proper lighting so that you can capture the best videos.

Build an audience

Next up, you have to increase your audience base. You have to create a big audience for yourself so that companies can approach you for affiliate marketing. You have to spoon-feed your audience every time to click on the like and the subscribe button. Aim to increase your audience by at least 100 per week so that you can turn your channel into a lucrative passive income outlet. Don't limit yourself to just your social media and get other people to promote you as well. That way, you can get their friends to like your channel and build a more significant audience base. It is now quite popular to feature in other people's videos or get a mention so that you can get some of their subscribers on board. Make sure you tie up with popular YouTubers to increase your viewership.

Affiliate marketing

As discussed in the previous chapter, affiliate marketing is all about tying up with companies to promote their products and services. If you have a popular channel, then companies will approach you and send you their products for review. You have to test out the product and give the audience your unbiased opinion so that you can build credibility. The more products you review, the more views you get and the more the companies that approach you.

Rewards and giveaways

To increase the number of viewers who visit your channel, you have to reward them and give away stuff. This giveaway can be free things that you get from your affiliate sponsors. You can host a competition such as answering simple questions or adding punch line and choose a random winner. You should also offer referral rewards such as discount coupons and other such lucrative prizes that will motivate people to draw in others.

Monetization

Next comes the monetization. Ad monetization can be achieved by signing up with Google AdWords and AdSense. AdWords and AdSense are two software owned by Google that are designed to play ads before a video on YouTube automatically. If you have watched a video on YouTube, then you would have noticed an ad playing first before the video starts. These ads are automatically played and chosen by Google. Whenever a person clicks on the ads, you stand to gain money from it. If the person places an order based on the click, then you will get a percentage of the sales value.

Both AdWords and AdSense are smart technologies and will know exactly what ads to play. For example, if your channel is all about reviewing children's toys then it will play ads of toys that people will be tempted to check out.

You have to have a minimum of $100 in your account to be able to cash on it and will be paid on the 15th of the month. You can wait longer if you wish to get paid a more significant sum and ask them to pay only after reaching a target such as $500 or $1,000.

Paid viewership

If in case your channel becomes very popular and you gain a lot of viewership then you can consider making a paid channel or paid subscription channel. As per this, people pay a certain sum to gain access to exclusive videos and content. As part of the offer, your audience will receive a free 14-day trial and then pay an amount to view the content.

Here are some tips to popularize your YouTube channel.

- Make sure you put up a video as often as possible ideally every other day. This is especially important to do if you have just started out and would like to increase your viewership.
- Google provides you with a statistical tool known as Google analytics that you can use to find out how popular your channel is doing and what are the videos that are making you more money. You

can use the data to enhance your channel's viewership.

- You have to provide a link to your YouTube channel on all your social media platforms. Make sure you explicitly remind people to visit, like and subscribe to your channel.

- Many YouTubers make the mistake of skipping weekends. You must not make this mistake and ensure that you put something up on Saturdays and Sundays as well.

Once your channel gets going, the possibilities are unlimited, and you can consider becoming a full-time YouTuber.

Chapter 4 Real Estate

Real estate is a booming business and one that can help you earn a decent passive income.

When it comes to real estate, most people assume that it is only about buying a house and renting it out. However, there are many other things that you can do with real estate. Some of them will be discussed in this chapter.

Buy/sell/rent houses

The traditional way of using real estate to earn a passive income is by buying a home and renting it out. By doing so, you stand a chance to put your money to work instead of keeping it locked up and earn money by way of rent or lease. If you have borrowed money for the purchase, then you can make up for it by receiving a monthly rent. When it comes to buying property, you can choose from individual houses, flats, villas, condos etc. Make sure you do your due research before buying so that you get your hands on the best property. A property in a good place with good facilities might cost you more but will also help you earn a better rent. You must also buy a property that will appreciate in value and not depreciate.

You can also consider investing in a commercial space that can be given away to offices and businesses. It will be easier for you to keep track of the activity that is going on and easier to find a replacement in case a company winds up and leaves.

There is also the concept of flipping where you buy a house, renovate it and sell it off immediately. This works well during distress sales where you can easily find properties that are selling for cheap. If you do not wish to go through the hassle of finding a home and renting it out, then you can consider investing in realty shares.

Realty shares are those that are designed to help in bringing together sellers, investors, and sponsors. It is used to help people set up a real estate fund and earn an income from it on a monthly basis. There are many real estate platforms to choose from, and you can go through all the options available before picking a lucrative one. For example, there will be some that exclusively focus on real estate deals where investors can choose properties to invest in their shares. These properties can range between condos, villas, resorts etc.

The world of realty shares is closely guarded and requires you to be part of an elite group of investors who have direct access to first-hand information. This information will be shared with investors through an intricate system to ensure that the right deal reaches the right investor.

One benefit of investing in such shares is that you need not worry if you do not have money ready to be invested immediately. You can borrow the money and buy the shares and then repay the money with interest once you start earning money from the shares. There will be many ready to lend the money at reasonable interest rates.

In fact, you need not collect the money and directly pay for the shares. Once your loan has been approved, you will be allotted shares. If you happen to be investing with a big and well-known company and the project turns out to be a success, then you might be given bonus shares or other rewards for your investment.

You can go through a broker to find you good deals if you do not have time on your hands to do your research. Once the agreement has been finalized, all you have to do is sit back and enjoy the rewards of your investment. It will grow in value over time and also help you earn a monthly sum. In time, you might even be able to buy the property in question.

Here are some criteria that should be met if you wish to invest in realty shares.

- You should have an annual income of $200,000 as an individual or $300,000 along with your spouse

- This should be your income for at least the last two years or 3 years if it is along with your spouse and are required to earn the same for the time to come
- You have a net worth of $1 million individually or with your spouse

These happen to be the criteria that have to be met in case you wish to invest in realty shares.

Chapter 5 Training Programs/ Art/ Dance/ Crafts

If you happen to be well versed in a specific skill such as dancing or singing, then you can use it to set up a passive income business.

Dancing/ singing/ aerobics/ yoga

You can make a YouTube channel to post tutorials of dancing, playing guitar, singing etc. you can also sign up with a club that is looking for teachers who can teach these skills.

One great way of capitalizing on the skill is by having your own studio or using your terrace or garage as a place to teach a hobby. If you are good at aerobics or yoga, then you can teach your audience moves and poses. You can dedicate just an hour each day to taking classes.

If you have a good singing voice, then you can create jingles for clients. Look up Fiverr and other such platforms that list singing jobs. It will take you only a little time to come up with a unique jingle and can create as many as you want.

Software/ apps

If you are an engineer or someone good at programming, then there are opportunities to create programs and software. You can find clients who need it for their companies. You will be given specific instructions that you have to follow to customize the software. You can also consider building apps and sell them on the Android or iOS store. Look for the latest trends and games and post them on the platforms.

Translating

If you are good in a language, then you can provide translation services. It can be translating from English to French, French to English, French to Spanish etc. you can choose whatever you are comfortable with. If you are well versed in the language, then consider becoming a tutor. Sign up with a website that offers students the chance to learn a language online. You might have to be present at specific times to go live or can record a lesson and upload it for students to access whenever they want. Apart from language, you can become a tutor in any subject that you are strong in. Be it math or science, you can sign up with a website that provides tutors the opportunity to find students.

Logos and artwork

If you are good at drawing, then you can find clients who require logo designs and other artwork. Look up on Fiverr to find such people and create the logos and designs for them. If you already have sample logos, then you can customize and modify it for them. The same extends to artwork that you can customize for your clients or come up with newer designs. You can take up as many projects as you like depending on how fast you can deliver the work.

Crafts

If you are good at making crafts, then you can make them in bulk and sell them. This can include paintings, clothes, accessories etc. Make a Facebook page and list out all your items there. People will be able to contact you for the price and other details. There is no limit to the number of pieces that you can make and sell. You can also consider selling it on your website.

Etsy

Etsy is a great place for you to sell your arts and crafts. It is designed specifically for people who wish to gain an audience for their creative work. You will find a ready audience for your work and be able to sell it easily. You can use your social media accounts and promotion platforms such as Pinterest to pin the products so that people can see it and buy it.

Amazon

If you do not fancy having your own website, then you can sell it on Amazon. Amazon makes it easy for sellers to sell their products and will cut only a small percentage of the sales. You can also consider reselling items on Amazon. Buy them in bulk on a website such as Alibaba.com and sell them on Amazon.

eBay

Just like Amazon, you can also sell on eBay. Although it is not as popular as Amazon, you will find a specific group of buyers looking for vintage items or rare items. You can go through your house and find such items that are no longer of use to you and list them. Through eBay global easy buy program, you will be able to ship it to any part of the world.

Conclusion

Thank you again for buying this book!

I hope this book was able to help you to get ideas about how to generate passive income.

The next step is to take action and set up your business. You have to choose one of these options and turn it into a passive business.

It might take a little time for you to get started and settle into it but it will get easier as you go. You have to remain determined and enthusiastic if you wish to make the business a success. Treat it like your day job for at least the first few months of getting started so that it becomes easier to settle in with it.

You can diversify and take up different businesses and not rely on a single business.

Finally, if you enjoyed this book, then I'd like to ask you for a favor, would you be kind enough to leave a review for this book on Amazon? It'd be greatly appreciated!

Thank you and good luck!

Preview of 'Freedom: How to Make Money Online and Become Financially Free by Creating Passive Income'

Before you can learn the specifics of building a passive income, it is critical that you understand what you are venturing into so that you don't start with a wrong idea of what it is you are working towards as well as what to expect from your efforts. Let's begin.

Passive Income: A Comprehensive Background

A passive income, also called a residual income, is simply the money you earn when you are not actively working. If you are actively working, it means you will receive some money (active income), which, when you stop working, you stop earning. With contract work or active work, you have to do some work to receive pay. In other words, you MUST exchange your time (hours, minutes, days, weeks or even months) for pay. In that case, if you are not working, you cannot be paid; it is simple logic!

This is always not the case with a passive income. With passive incomes, you earn whether you work actively or not. To create a passive income stream, you will have to put in some work upfront to get the ball rolling. You will however get to a point where your income stream will become passive such that it generates revenue on its own without you having to work for it. Think of publishing a book on Amazon for instance. After doing the upfront work of writing and promoting the book in its initial stages, you will get to a point whereby the book can continue making money whether you do anything to promote it or not. That's passive income!

Before we head any further, we have to discuss some things about a passive income because these things are important and will help you understand the nature of a passive income. Some of these include:

1: *Passive incomes are often not permanent incomes:* Get it right: some online passive incomes may last for years, decades, or even centuries. They can however never be permanent. This is because all forms of income eventually dry up at a given point for one reason or another.

2: *It is not a one-time lump sum payment:* Some incomes such as inheritance, sale of assets like pieces of land, or sale of stocks are one-time lump sum payments. This is not the case with passive income since a passive income is a source of income that has a sense of continuity over a certain period.

3: *Some passive incomes are semi-passive:* You may be your own boss but you will need to do some work (even if its management), although you will not receive pay for maintaining your investment.

For instance, if you build a house and rent it out, you will definitely receive your passive income from the tenants but when they move out, you will have to invest some energy, money, and time to maintain the vacated premise and seek other tenants.

4: Passive income streams need maintenance: Whether it is checking emails or paying taxes on your passive income, you have to do some of these activities for maintenance since they keep your source of passive income going.

5: Your passive income might be another person's active Income: No matter what kind of online business you invest in, you will have to hire people to do some work that help you earn your passive income. In other words, your passive income builds on leveraging on other people's active income to succeed! For example, if you have a freelance writing marketplace for instance, you will have to hire some people who will be writing or editing your articles. You will have to pay them hence they will receive active income but their work is what shall help you earn a passive income.

Now that we have established these critical things about passive income streams, the next thing we have to consider is why the internet is the best way to create multiple passive income streams.

Check out the rest of 'Freedom: How to Make Money Online and Become Financially Free by Creating Passive Income' on Amazon.

Or go to: **http://amzn.to/2nTo8oC**

Check Out My Other Books

Below you'll find some of my other popular books that are popular on Amazon and Kindle as well. Simply search for these titles on the Amazon website to find them. Alternatively, you can visit my author page on Amazon to see other work done by me.

Ketogenic Cookbook: Quick Low Calorie Ketogenic Crockpot Recipes with 7 Days Meal Plan

Freedom: How to Make Money Online and Become Financially Free by Creating Passive Income

Mediterranean Diet: Instant Pot Cookbook with Delicious Recipes

Alice the Superbug

Madison and Astrid's first magical journey

Intermittent Fasting: The Essential Beginners Guide for Women for Weight Loss

Chakra Healing: Chakra Healing and Karmic Awareness for Beginners

SEO 2017 for Growth: The Ultimate Guide to Learn Search Engine Optimization with Internet Marketing Tips

Psychology: How to Analyze People Using Human Psychological Techniques, Body Language Signals, Social Skills and Personality Types

Paleo Smoothies: Recipes to Energize and for Ultimate Health and Weight Loss

Belly Diet Smoothies: Delicious Smoothie Recipes to Flatten Your Belly, Improve Your Gut & Burn Fat

Keto Diet: Keto Diet Guide Cookbook for Beginners with Meal Plan and Simple, Delicious Recipes to Lose Weight and Look Good

Online Business from Scratch: The 9 Step Guide to Building a Profitable and Sustainable Online Business

Weight Loss: 20 Easy And Fast Diet Tips For Losing Weight - An Easy-To-Follow Weight Loss Guide

Ketogenic Cookbook: Ketogenic Cookbook for Beginners with 7 Days Meal Plan

Negative Calorie Diet: Cookbook & Guide Which Will Help You To Burn Body Fat, Lose Weight And Live Healthy

Negative Calorie Diet with Anti-Inflammatory Diet Guide

Make Money Online To Achieve Freedom

Negative Calorie Diet with Smart Fat Guide

Negative Calorie Diet & Clean Eating: Cookbook & Guide Which Will Help You To Burn Body Fat, Lose Weight And Live Healthy

Smart Fat: Cookbook with Fat Meals Which Help You to Lose Weight, Get Healthy and Improve Brain Function

Anti-Inflammatory Diet Guide: The Guide to Reduce Inflammation and Live a Healthy Life Without Pain

Essential Oils: The Young Living Book Guide of Natural Remedies for Beginners for Pets, For Dogs

Clean Eating: Cookbook and Guide to Restore Your Body's Natural Balance and Eat Healthy

Anti-Inflammatory Diet Guide: The Guide to Reduce Inflammation and Live a Healthy Life Without Pain

Dash Diet: Cookbook for Weight Loss with Action Plan and Easy Recipes

Air Fryer Cookbook: Quick, Healthy and Easy Low Carb Air Fryer Recipes

Psychology & Habits Of Highly Effective People Box Set

Leptin Resistance: Leptin Diet to Control Your Hormones, Get Permanent

Weight Loss, Cure Obesity and Live Healthy

Negative Calorie Diet & Dash Diet Box Set

Negative Calorie Diet & Weight Loss Box Set

Habits of Highly Effective People: What Are the Habits of Successful People?

Slow Cooker: Cookbook with Slow Cooker Recipes

Weight Loss Cookbook: Meal Prep Cookbook for Weight Loss and Clean Eating

Weight Loss Cookbook: Mediterranean Diet for Lasting Weight Loss

Negative Calorie Diet & Dash Diet Box Set

Slow Cooker & Instant Pot Box Set

Children Books: Madison and Astrid's first magical journey & Alice the Superbug Box Set

Belly Diet: The Zero Belly Diet Step-By-Step Guide Which Helps You to Lose Your Belly and Enjoy Your Flat Belly

Weight Loss: 20 Easy and Fast Diet Tips for Losing Weight - An Easy-To-Follow Weight Loss Guide

Instant Pot: Instant Pot Pressure Cooker Cookbook with Easy and Healthy Recipes

Bonus: Subscribe To The Free Enhance Your Business Report!

When you subscribe to Freedom Destination via email, you will get free access to a report. All you have to do is enter your email address to get instant access.

This report is going to discuss 10 important, and possible crucial facts/ideas that if implemented, will increase your business as well as your profits.

You can access it here: http://bit.ly/2tXwgKQ

www.ingramcontent.com/pod-product-compliance
Lightning Source LLC
Chambersburg PA
CBHW071240220526
45468CB00002B/943